Stress-Proof
Your Marriage

Stress-Proof Your Marriage

Cory and Heidi Busse

Our Sunday Visitor Publishing Division
Our Sunday Visitor, Inc.
Huntington, Indiana 46750

Nihil Obstat: Rev. Michael Heintz, Ph.D.
Censor Librorum
Imprimatur: ✠ John M. D'Arcy
Bishop of Fort Wayne-South Bend
September 22, 2009

Write:
Our Sunday Visitor Publishing Division
Our Sunday Visitor, Inc.
200 Noll Plaza
Huntington, IN 46750
1-800-348-2440
bookpermissions@osv.com

ISBN: 978-1-59276-707-6   (Inventory No. T1028)
LCCN: 2009936194

Cover design by Rebecca J. Heaston
Interior design by Sherri L. Hoffman

PRINTED IN THE UNITED STATES OF AMERICA

Contents

Introduction

A successful marriage requires falling in love many times, always with the same person.

— MIGNON McLaughlin

The great marriage myth of our time is that happy marriages "just happen." When we were first married, we — like many couples — were under the impression that true love was all that was required to live happily ever after. We certainly didn't believe that we needed to put any work into our marriage, because only unhappy couples "work on their marriages." We were in love, and love conquers all. Truly good marriages are always blissful and easy. We had it made.

Wow, were *we* wrong.

The images of love and marriage today reinforce the idea that real love is easy, and experiencing hardship means you've married the wrong person. So we break up or divorce and remarry in hopes of finding an easier love, a perfect love. The reality is that we are still human beings struggling to find our way through relationships. We make mistakes. We let each other down. We fail. We fight. We sin.

The story of creation reminds us that, while we were created in the image and likeness of God (Gen 1:27), we are not gods ourselves. We're human beings with a great capacity for good, but also the capacity for evil.

When God discovers that Adam and Eve have eaten of the tree of life, we are reminded of our human-ness and imperfection:

> Then the LORD God said, "Behold, the man has become like one of us, knowing good and evil; and now, lest he put forth his hand and take also of the tree of life, and eat, and live for ever" — therefore the LORD God sent him forth from the garden of Eden.
>
> — GEN 3:22-23

And so, from the beginning, it was foretold that human beings would know both good times and bad, sickness and health, and that there'd even be a "till-death-do-us-part" part. Humanity's first couple getting evicted from the Garden of Eden should've been our first clue that marriage wasn't going to be easy!

Difficult times visit every marriage. Unexpected challenges arise: illness, job loss, or death in the family. You'll face your own crises. But that doesn't mean your marriage is doomed. Far from it.

We hope this book will help strengthen your marriage so that when life's challenges happen, your marriage will bend, not break. We feel qualified to give marital advice not because our marriage has been perfect, but because we've had our own challenges.

Just as no marriage is a constant honeymoon, it's not all gloom and dirty dishes, either. We don't pretend to have "The Answers," but we do believe a good reminder of the right questions to ask will give you tools to find *your* answers — the ones that will help your marriage.

CHAPTER 1

Talk

Jesus Spoke in Parables. You Probably Shouldn't.

> *The great enemy of clear language is insincerity.*
> — GEORGE ORWELL

Everyone tells couples that *communication* is one of the most important elements of any relationship. The irony is, the advice usually stops there. Ask most people for more concrete examples of good communication techniques, and there is a lot of hedging and head-scratching.

Listen

The most common misconception about communication is that it is about being *heard*. About being *understood*. In other words, it's about *talking*. It isn't. At least not 50 percent of it. When in doubt, look back to the Prayer of Saint Francis:

> O Divine Master,
> Grant that I may not so much seek to be...
> understood, as to understand.

The best communicators know when to stop talking. Marital communication isn't a presidential debate. Good communicators do not cross their arms and impatiently tap a mental foot and latch on to the one weak point in their spouse's argument that they can exploit and turn to their advantage.

- Listening means being open.
- Listening means seeking to understand where our spouse is coming from.
- Listening means paying attention.

Whether remembering an important upcoming appointment or understanding which subjects are best avoided at Christmas dinner, careful, attentive listening can go a long way toward avoiding stress in a marriage.

> *Courage is what it takes to stand up and speak; courage is also what it takes to sit down and listen.*
> — WINSTON CHURCHILL

Say What You Mean; Mean What You Say

Emotion plays a big part in communication (and an even bigger part in *mis*communication). Sentiments important to one person that are not treated importantly by another lead to hurt feelings at best. At worst, they sow the seeds of lingering resentment.

That's why one good way to alleviate stress in a marriage is to **keep communication simple**. Metaphor and simile, poetry and cliché all have their place in marital communications. But when what we're saying has to be absolutely, positively clear, it's best to get right to the point. "Say it plain," as the saying goes.

Sometimes this means having periods of silence while we work out the complicated alchemy that converts emotions and thoughts into words. And that's okay. It can be a struggle to compose clear language when we're on the spot. And impatient prompting only clouds the process.

Here are some starters that can keep conversation simple and straightforward:

"It is important to me that . . . "

"What I'd like to see happen is . . ."

"When I'm in that situation, I feel . . ."

"Something I've considered that might help is . . ."

And don't forget to check in frequently. A sincere "Does what I've said make sense?" gives your spouse the chance to question, challenge, and get a word in edgewise.

Ask for What You Want

Related to clear communication is another very simple tactic toward stopping stress in its tracks: ask for what you want.

Choices about how many children to raise, where to live, and how to save and spend money are things best discussed and agreed upon mutually. More day-to-day decisions in a marriage don't carry so much weight. Unilateral decisions are sometimes okay, and one half of the equation genuinely may not have a preference.

Ironically, though, *these* are the times when not asking for what we want leads to avoidable stress in a marriage. Ask yourself: how often have we been involved in this kind of a conversation?

A: Where do you want to (go, eat, sit, vacation, live)?

B: Wherever. It doesn't really matter to me.

A: How about (a movie, our favorite restaurant, the fourth row, Paris, the suburbs)?

B: Sure. That's fine. (Disappointment and resentment fester because I had a preference and never expressed it.)

Stress arises when we *do* have opinions but, because we're torn or lazy or feeling responsible for the weight of the decision, we end up not expressing them and then find ourselves disappointed in the outcome. Often, an expression of one opinion shakes us loose from a list of equal options to a process of elimination that can lead to greater satisfaction all around.

This does not mean that we can all be divas and demand our way. But if you have a preference, give voice to it. And when things don't go our way... well, there's a chapter on fighting later in this book.

Great minds discuss ideas; average minds discuss events; small minds discuss people.

— ELEANOR ROOSEVELT

Rough Spots

Communication styles among couples are as different as couples themselves. Some spouses thrive on small talk, but others seem perfectly happy chewing their eggs in silence. Some never seem to be on the same page, while others finish one another's sentences. The point is, finding your communication style takes some trial and (unfortunately) error.

Here are a few habits that are almost guaranteed to cause a "failure to communicate."

Family Feud. It's one thing if *I* express frustration about my family, but it's off limits for *you* to do it.

White Noise. It's not as if every conversation has to be about the Gnostic Gospels, but try to be intentional in conversation. Running commentary tends to get drowned out, and somebody's feelings inevitably get hurt.

Broadcasting. Check with your spouse before you dive into that anecdote that was really funny at the time; it may not be so funny in mixed company. And when in doubt, shut up.

Take Away

The goal of healthy marital communication is to be understood. Speak clearly; listen to each other; and ask for what you want.

CHAPTER 2

Touch

Seriously, the Catholic Church Wants You To.

Millions and millions of years would still not give me half enough time to describe that tiny instant of all eternity when you put your arms around me and I put my arms around you.

— JACQUES PRÉVER

Our need for human contact is essential. Studies show that babies who are not touched do not develop properly. The same is true for adults. Human touch has been shown to have a positive effect on healing, grieving, even depression.

Dr. Tiffany Field of the Touch Research Institute at the University of Miami has found that touching can have a medicinal effect. The Institute examines the body's reaction to external stimulation (like a hug). Recent studies have shown that human touch can help:

- alleviate depression symptoms
- reduce physical pain
- reduce stress
- improve immune function

"Hugging and massages and doing various forms of exercise stimulate pressure receptors," she explains. "It slows down heart rate and blood pressure and the production of stress hormones."

In marriage, touch helps keep two people close. Both sexual and nonsexual touch is important. Touch is a way to create and keep intimacy alive in marriage, and it's especially vital for a couple working through a stressful time. Hugs, hand-holding, shoulder rubs, and other forms of intimate touch help couples feel secure and communicate messages in a way that words cannot. Touch can convey messages such as, "You're not alone" or "I'm sorry" in times when words fall short.

Some of us come from families where hugs were a normal part of our everyday lives, while others grew up with almost no physical contact from parents and siblings. How we were raised will certainly have an effect on how comfortable we are with touch in marriage.

How you connect physically is not nearly as important as how often you touch one another in a loving way. Hugs and kisses shouldn't be reserved for special occasions like your anniversary. Kiss your spouse goodbye every morning. We learned this lesson through tragedy. A family member left for work one morning. His wife was sleeping so soundly, he didn't wake her to kiss her goodbye. Later that day, she had a heart attack and passed away. He's regretted that morning ever since.

Talking about Touching

While the Catholic Church has a reputation for being prudish about touch, in fact, the Church teaches that conjugal love is an integral part of marriage and essential to the permanence of the bond, and thus one of the essential properties of marriage itself (Canon 1061). Put another way, not only does Catholicism encourage sex in a marriage, it's *required*. (And nobody likes a rule breaker, so...)

Our sexuality is a gift from God to be given as a gift to our spouse. Sexual intercourse, when offered out of free and total love and fidelity for another person, is the ultimate reflection of the marital bond. Changes in sexual behavior are often first signs that there are problems in a marriage or that a couple is feeling disconnected from one another.

Many couples fall into the myth that good marital sex "just happens" (it doesn't), and it will always be just like it is in the movies. Well, we're here to tell you that real life isn't Hollywood. (For one thing, in real life, you're required to do your own stunts.) In the real world, it's important for couples to talk about how they like to be touched, both sexually and nonsexually. Spouses are not mind readers. What may bring one spouse comfort and pleasure may be annoying for the other.

Human skin is like a field of grass, each blade a nerve ending so sensitive that the slightest graze can etch into the human brain a memory of the moment.

— HELEN FISHER

Below are some talking points to help encourage conversation about touch:

- What is your favorite (nonsexual) way to be touched?
- What kind of touch makes you feel safe?
- Is there any kind of touch that you do not like? (e.g., tickling)
- Is the family you grew up in comfortable with touch? Did you grow up with a lot of hugs?

- How do we incorporate touch into our family when we have kids?

Hands Off

Of course, there are times when we don't want to be touched. During these times, it's really important to let your spouse know in a gentle and loving way that you are still very much in love with them, but that a scalp massage might not be particularly welcome while we're cleaning the fish tank. Or if you've been with the kids all day, you may need a break from all physical touch after being climbed on, spit-up on, wrestled with . . .

We've found that when things escalate and one or both of you is about to say or do something you may regret, touching is a great way to break the tension. Many times, we've forced ourselves to stop talking and hold hands for two minutes in the middle of a fight. It feels really strange in the moment, and it doesn't solve the conflict or take away the anger. But it does remind us that we are on the same team and, even though we disagree, we do so from a place of love.

Take Away

Talking about touching is as important as touch itself.

CHAPTER 3

Share

The Best Things in Life Are Free . . .

> *Forty-nine percent of women say it's easier to talk to your husband about sex than money.*
> — *PARENTING* MAGAZINE POLL, AUGUST 2009

The one subject we still get squirrelly talking about is money. We get uncomfortable talking about how much we have. We can be equally uncomfortable talking about how much we don't have. Or how much we want. Or what we do with it when we do have it. (One of the biggest fights of my sister's marriage was over what she and her husband would do if they won $1 million from the McDonald's "Monopoly" promotion.)

Money is another area in marriage where platitudes are common and genuine advice is hard to come by. Usually, this is because we have our own hang-ups about money. And although money worries are often unavoidable, the marital stresses they bring with them aren't.

Talk Turkey

It's hard to talk about money; and although talking about money, especially in this economy, seems inevitable, it isn't. A June 2009 Associated Press article reported that only 45 percent of married couples make decisions together about day-to-day finances. And only 38 percent discussed how they should invest for their retirement.[1]

The good news: if you and your spouse don't talk about money, you're not alone. The bad news: money is the #1 cause of stress in a marriage. So swallow hard and talk seriously about money. For the great majority of us, the conversation isn't about whether or not we should buy the yacht or the private jet, but sweeping financial concerns and aspirations under the rug leads to resentment, secrets, and unnecessary competition for what are often scarce resources.

Important lessons come out of these conversations. From them, we learn from our spouses whether we're spenders or savers, whether we have simple desires or "champagne dreams and caviar wishes." And we can divine who should manage the family finances. (In some cases, the answer is "neither of us," and that leads to another conversation about whether or not it's okay to ask a third party to help. Hint: it is.)

The important thing is to talk about money. Talk a lot, if that's what is necessary. Here are some conversation starters:

- What kind of lifestyle do you want to live?
- What are your financial priorities and goals?
- How do you feel about debt?
- Are you more likely to save for something you want, or do you spend a lot on impulse buys?
- What would we do about money if one of us lost our job or got really sick?

---

1. "Putting Out Fires Without Planning for the Future." Associated Press. June 11, 2009. http://www.msnbc.msn.com/id/31261032/ (Referenced July 20, 2009).

- How much do you think we should give to our (church? charities? retirement fund?)
- What would we do with an extra $500 a month?

My Emotional Baggage Isn't Designer

We attach a lot of emotion to money. While talking about money, don't ignore the emotions the conversation brings up in you.

Fear in conversations about money is often related to underlying scarcity issues. Fear of not having "enough" (whatever that means to us). Fear of losing what we do have. Fear is a common emotion. Getting honest about money fears is key to helping spouses understand our worries.

Envy is an unattractive emotion. As Catholics, we're taught that "coveting" is a serious sin. More often than not, envy has us believing that what we have equates to what we are worth. Denying how we feel won't help us overcome the problems resulting from those feelings. Owning up to envy helps us get at what "keeping up with the Joneses" really brings up in us, and it lets our spouse reassure us that we are more than what we own.

And the man and his wife were both naked and were not ashamed.

— GEN 2:25

Shame is a natural emotion that keeps us human. It can also be the most self-destructive emotion we have. When we feel shame in relation to money ("I don't feel like I deserve it" or "I could have done something 'better' with this money" or "I can't afford to give my kids

21

the kind of life I want to"), we're really putting more value on money than on the lives and relationships it is meant to enhance. Talk about shame, and don't let it eat you (and your marriage) up.

"Budget" Is a Six-Letter Word, Not Four

It's one of the most common pieces of advice. It's tossed out as if it's the easiest thing in the world. "First, sit down and create a budget."

Yeah. Right.

Ask anyone who has worked in an office what the *worst* part of their job is, and the answer will probably be: budgeting. Budgeting is hard. There's a lot of guess-work. And it's not very fun. There are always, *always* more priorities than there is money.

At the same time, it can also be an extremely hopeful and liberating exercise.

Budgeting is making the choice to take your marriage's head out of the financial sand. Budgeting is about acknowledging where the money goes and making changes (if need be). Budgeting is about working together.

That's all well and good, but how the heck do you start?

A good first step is Phil Lenahan's *7 Steps to Becoming Financially Free* (Our Sunday Visitor Publishing). But to get you started budgeting, try this:

Get your bills from last month. All of them. Add them up to find your expenses. Talk about areas you think are legitimate and where you might be putting money that could be better spent (saved or invested) elsewhere.

Rigorously track your spending — every penny — for a month. You'll be shocked at where it goes.

If you bank online, you probably have access to software that will show where your money's going. It will also help you budget and plan for upcoming expenses. Quickenonline.com has a free account that will show you trends, set goals, and even budget by expense category (Groceries, Gas, Entertainment).

If you're more of a do-it-yourselfer, there are loads of budget spreadsheet templates available for Microsoft Excel.

Value what you value. Don't let expenses be arbitrary. Give to your church and charities (10 percent). Save for a rainy day and retirement (15 percent). Pay bills, and live on what's left. Attaching value to giving, saving, and spending makes your financial choices intentional.

The point is less about subtracting what you save, spend, or invest from what you earn and more about agreeing on priorities.

Dirty (Not-So) Little Secrets

If there is one piece of advice newly married (and not-so newly married) couples should take, it is that there should be complete transparency on money matters. Hiding debt, disguising purchases, and making "sure-thing" investments without the knowledge or consent of our spouses is not okay.

We maintain separate checking accounts. But early in our marriage, we agreed that we'd discuss any purchase over $50. When we got established and had children, we joked about how we could spend $50 on a small box of diapers and single can of formula. But we'd established a solid foundation of trust and consent in our marriage. We weren't asking permission; we were respecting that we were in our marriage together, and that means taking care of our family finances is a mutual responsibility.

Take Away

Talking about goals, budgets, and the emotions money brings up is like money in the bank.

CHAPTER 4

Fight

When in Doubt, Have It Out.

> *Anger ventilated often hurries toward forgiveness; and concealed often hardens into revenge.*
> — EDWARD G. BULWER-LYTTON

True or False: Happy couples never fight.

If you said "True," there's good news and bad news. The bad news is you're wrong. The good news is you're in good company.

The reason we *think* that happy couples never fight is that we seldom see couples fight. Moreover, when we *do* see others fight, it makes us uncomfortable. It feels too private. Too intimate to be aired in the open. We grow up with our parents admonishing us, "Don't fight." Our advice is different: Fight. It's good for your marriage.

Fighting can be like a release valve. Fighting about big stuff like sex, money, and children can seem cliché. But just because these fights are common doesn't make them unimportant.

Just as often, though, fights about the "little things" are the ones that can be the haymakers. Fights about family, friends, jobs, attention, housework, habits — and the million other things that s/he always does that make us crazy — are the ones that can be kept small if done well. Rather than letting frustrations and irritations build up to the point where things are grave and differences are irreconcilable, giving voice to them before they have a chance to spiral out of control can save a lot of wear and tear on a marriage.

What Fighting Is NOT

There are some rules. Effective fighting is rooted in love and a genuine desire for reconciliation. With that in mind, let's start with a few definitions of what effective fighting is not...

Abuse. It is never okay for a fight to become physically or emotionally abusive. If it does — if it even *seems like it might* — get help immediately. Get family, friends, your priest, the police, a counselor, *someone* to intervene.

Bickering. We all know the couple that bickers constantly. It's a constant battle to one-up the other. That's not the kind of fighting that is good for a marriage. It's petulant. It's immature. And it has a way of infecting other people. If couples around you bicker, it is perfectly acceptable to leave them in the parking lot.

Nagging. There's a difference between having a legitimate axe to grind and just being a scold. If *everything* your spouse does annoys you, the problem may not be with your spouse. Then again, it may be... but it's worth a second look.

Cheap Shots and Hot Buttons. It's impossible to tell couples that they should never be angry or defensive or hurt or cornered when they fight. In those situations, it's really tempting to try to "win." Remember, though, that when one of you *wins* a fight, you both lose. The goal of any fight is not to win, it's to find common ground. It's not to make our spouse hurt or feel bad, it's to find a situation where everyone gets to feel good.

Come Out Fighting

Here are five strategies for effective fighting:

1) *Assume Positive Intent.*

Don't get defensive. Give your spouse the benefit of the doubt. In her book *The Truth About Love: The Highs, the Lows, and How You Can Make It Last Forever,* author Pat Love (no kidding) tells couples, "If you look behind criticism, you will find a desire." In other words, if you can keep from getting defensive and give your spouse the benefit of the doubt, you'll probably find the genuine desire for reconciliation rooted in love. Love cites, for example, that the spouse who complains, "You never want to spend time with me!" is really saying that they want to spend time with their spouse. Work hard to discover the real reason for a fight, and assume the reason for the fight is positive.

2) *Respect Personality Types.*

A common misperception is that "introverts" are shy and "extroverts" are gregarious. Being classified an introvert or an extrovert often has less to do with where you spend time at a party and more to do with how you process information. A very loose interpretation of the Meyers-Briggs Type Indicator (MBTI) is to say that extroverts process out loud while introverts think and then talk. If you and your spouse have differing personality types, you're going to fight in different ways. Be mindful of how your spouse processes and makes decisions. Extroverts should be careful not to "ambush" introverted spouses. Introverts should remember that an extroverted spouse may not have put concrete words around what is bothering them before they began speaking.

3) *It's Never "Always" or "Never."*

The words "always" and "never" are seldom helpful to conversation. Hasty generalizations like "You always _____" or "You never _____" are phrases designed to win a fight, not to help it toward resolution. No one "always" does something or "never" does another. When we hear ourselves saying these words, it's time to stop and rephrase. Again, refer to #1 above and dig into what the fight is really about.

4) *Stick with It.*

A common desire in the midst of a fight is to quit on it too soon. Some of us storm off in the middle of a fight (Leaving). Others give in to keep from having to fight in the first place (Ducking). Still others disengage, nod, and give noncommittal "uh-huhs" until our spouse loses interest (Playing Possum). With any of these tendencies, "living to fight another day" only prolongs the inevitable. Remember, the goal of effective fighting is to get at problems early (and often, if necessary). Going all fifteen rounds isn't about defending yourself, it's about defending your marriage.

5) *It's Not a Spectator Sport.*

It's probably best to keep your fights private. Even when we follow all the rules, it's impossible for others to truly understand. It's human nature to take sides, make judgments, gossip, and hold grudges, and those things will only add stress to your marriage. That's not to say that venting or confiding or getting help and support in tough times isn't perfectly okay. Keep in mind, though, that it's your marriage and your fight; don't give your friends, family, or kids ringside seats.

Forgive, and forgive, and forgive. When it's over and the fight is done, forgive one another. "Seventy times seven" times, as Jesus told Peter. Sometimes that forgiveness won't come right away, but even in those circumstances, it's important not to hold forgiveness hostage or withhold it like a punishment.

A happy marriage is the union of two good forgivers.
— RUTH BELL GRAHAM

Take Away

Get good at fighting effectively; then, get even better at forgiving.

CHAPTER 5

Pray

The Couple That Prays Together . . . Well . . .
You Know the Rest.

> *Pray always.*
> — 1 THESS 5:16

Do you pray together? It's a question that is rarely asked in marriage preparation classes and almost certainly never asked of a couple who has been married for several years. In some circles there is an embarrassment about prayer, as if admitting to praying somehow makes us weak or silly. Nothing could be further from the truth. Recent studies show that praying together is a leading indicator for a lasting marriage.

St. Paul encourages us to "pray always." Of course, he doesn't mean that we should always be engaged in formal prayer (saying the rosary while operating heavy machinery tends to make some people uneasy). What St. Paul is reminding us is that prayer must be integral to our daily lives as Christians. Prayer is our central way of communicating with God. Talking to God together as a couple is a way of acknowledging God's presence in the marriage.

But let's be honest. For many of us, praying is usually a private endeavor or something we do with our kids. How in the world are we supposed to pray with our spouse? If you have never prayed together, it may feel strange at first. But take the leap. Before you begin, remember that prayer is a time when we express our deepest needs and wants, our most innate fears and our most charitable thoughts. You will learn a great deal about each other through prayer. It is important to feel safe with each other so that you're comfortable expressing your honest feelings.

Praying can strengthen your bond with your spouse and increase satisfaction in your marriage. Shared prayer helps us realize that much of life is beyond our control. Especially during challenging times — loss of a job, a death or illness in the family, a child who is struggling — it is important to share our feelings with each other and with God.

> *God tells us to burden Him with whatever burdens us.*
> — AUTHOR UNKNOWN

Pray Always . . . or At Least Pray Sometimes.

Below are some ideas on when and how to integrate prayer into your marriage.

Before Going to Sleep at Night.

Try praying out loud together at bedtime. Turn off the light and appreciate the silence. Then talk to God out loud. Together. You are likely to feel incredibly vulnerable praying with your spouse the first few times, and that's okay. Start off easy: thank God for the blessings of the day. When you're ready, talk to God about your hopes and anxieties for the future.

Before Meals — Even in Restaurants.

What is it about our culture that frowns upon prayer in public places? Be daring. When you're out together on a date (or even at a restaurant for a family dinner) say a short prayer thanking God for the great gift of food. It doesn't have to be long or fancy or loud. You're not praying for show. A simple, "Thank you God for this food and the love at this table" is what we often say. At home, praying before meals is a daily reminder of the divine presence in daily life.

During Housework.

Okay, this idea may seem farfetched, but it really helps to bring the mundane tasks of housecleaning to a new level. Thank God for the "blessed mess" of your home (especially if you have kids) and know that God is with you in chaos.

> *It doesn't have to be solemn to be sacred.*
> — RABBI DAVID WOLPE

Before You Part Each Day.

Start a new tradition. Before leaving for work each morning, share a short blessing with your spouse before you kiss goodbye. Something short like, "May the Lord bless your day" or "May God be with you today." As Catholics, even a simple, "Peace be with you," is a familiar way to welcome God into your day-to-day lives.

Pray with the Psalms.

The Book of Psalms was written for the purpose of ancient prayer and liturgical worship. If you haven't read it (and, being Catholic, you're not alone if you haven't), it's a beautiful expression of poetry and prayer and human emotion. The word "psalm" is a Greek word that, loosely translated, means "song sung to the music of a harp or lyre." The psalms were the "light rock" of biblical times. There are psalms of thanksgiving, of praise, and of lament. It's especially helpful to turn to the Psalms in stressful times. The next time you're feeling down or overwhelmed, try reading a psalm out loud to each other before bed. Psalm 126 is a reminder that everything, all of our joys and sorrows, are from God.

> The Lord has done great things for us;
>   we are glad.
> Restore our fortunes, O Lord,
>   like the watercourses in the Negeb!
> May those who sow in tears
>   Reap with shouts of joy!
> He that goes forth weeping,
>   bearing the seed for sowing,
> shall come home with shouts of joy,
> bringing his sheaves with him.
>
> — Ps 126:3-6

God speaks in the silence of the heart.
Listening is the beginning of prayer.
— MOTHER TERESA

You Don't Have a Prayer . . . Or Do You?

Sometimes, words aren't enough to express our deepest needs or our heartfelt sympathy and consolation. Simply sitting together in silence can be a prayer. For many couples today, life is so busy and filled with noise, that silence can easily be mistaken for boredom. We are conditioned to feel like we should be doing something every minute. It is important, however, to embrace quiet time together and allow some room in your marriage to listen for God's voice. Some ways to embrace silence together:

- Turn off the car radio on your next date night and spend some quiet time in prayer.
- Get up early some Saturday morning (before the kids — this will be a challenge) and watch the sunrise together over coffee.
- Sit on the front stoop after the kids are in bed and look at the stars together (bonus: good excuse to cuddle in a blanket together).

Take Away

Find the ways that you feel comfortable praying as a couple and see how God helps transform your marriage.

CHAPTER 6

Worship

Sing Alleluia! (Even If It's Out of Tune.)

> *Marriage is an act of will that signifies and involves a*
> *mutual gift, which unites the spouses and binds them*
> *to their eventual souls, with whom they make up a sole*
> *family — a domestic church.*
>
> — POPE JOHN PAUL II

When you're dating or newly married, it is easy to get into your own little world where all you need is each other and no one else. We joke that the early days of love (or better yet, infatuation) should be called "living on a Cert" because all you need is a breath mint and your spouse to be happy. Of course, as time passes it becomes clear that two people cannot be absolutely everything to each other and that you will need to rely on some form of community to thrive as a couple.

The Catholic Church teaches that at our baptism we not only start a *personal* relationship with Jesus Christ, we are also welcomed into the full community of believers — the Church. We believe that human beings were created with a deeply rooted need for God and for each other. Indeed, other human beings can be reflections of the divine presence here on earth.

An October 2008 American Psychological Association study on the effects of stress in America found that attending church services is the second most effective form of stress management in this country. The first? Prayer. And, because the Catholic Mass is the central form of communal prayer for the Church, it would seem to be quite effective at helping to manage stress.

Weave in faith and God will find the thread.
— AUTHOR UNKNOWN

There is great comfort and security in the ritual of going to Mass together; it's a weekly reminder that we are involved in something greater than ourselves. Throughout the weeks and months, the Church celebrates the various seasons in the life of Christ. Celebrating these seasons at church as well as in your home is another way to strengthen your bond and become a "family of faith."

Attending Mass together as a married couple will strengthen your relationship with Christ as well as with one another.

Eat Together. The Eucharist (Communion) is a sacrificial meal. Much like our Thanksgiving holiday, our church family gathers each week to pray, share the sacred story (Scripture readings), forgive one another, and partake in the Eucharistic meal. (In fact, *Eucharist* means "thanksgiving.") Jesus left us the Eucharist as a way to experience his real presence in our lives long after he had risen. Receiving Communion together as a couple brings Christ into your marriage in a literal way.

Be Changed. You may not realize it, but attending Mass is transformative. Okay, so the homily may not always be riveting and an out-of-tune cantor might mean that the music isn't always angelic. The Risen Christ is always fully present in the Catholic liturgy in four specific ways:

1. in the Priest
2. in the Word
3. in the Eucharistic "species" (bread and wine)
4. in the people (us)

It's true. Not only are the bread and wine changed into the Body of Christ; so are we. And once changed, we're sent out into the world, and we're expected to be Christ for one another.

Hear the Story. Attending Mass is a great way to hear the sacred story of our faith. Hearing the Word proclaimed at church is a reminder that our faith tradition was meant to be shared with other believers. Listening to the Gospels together as a couple (and as a family) helps to integrate Jesus' teachings into daily life. Talk about the message of the Gospel on your ride home from Mass or over coffee after church. Sacred scripture has a way of teaching us about each other ... and ourselves.

Lean on Me. Or more specifically, lean on "us." If you're facing life challenges or difficulties in your marriage, allow your parish community to prop you up through those tough times. Talk with your pastor, deacon, or pastoral care minister and let them know that you need the community's prayers and support. Spending time with parishioners who have been married for many years is also a great way to learn about life's ups and downs.

Have a Good Week. Aside from the theological and spiritual reasons, there is a very practical reason to attend

Mass: it gets your week off to a great start. Going to Mass reminds us of what's important and grounds us in those things that matter — faith, family, and friends.

Take Away

People who attend church are happier and healthier, and manage stress better, than those who do not.

CHAPTER 7

Eat

You Don't Have to Turn Water Into Wine.
(But It Can't Hurt.)

> *We should look for someone to eat and drink with before looking for something to eat and drink.*
>
> — EPICURUS

Numerous recent studies show that eating together has a positive effect on our health and well-being. According to one survey,[1] frequent family meals are related to better nutritional intake and a decreased risk for unhealthy weight control practices and substance abuse.

Eating together is valuable because it connects us as a couple and binds us together as a family. In our busy, overstressed lives, sitting down to eat is a time to stop, unwind, check-in.

Jesus is a model for sharing meals with people. The Gospels show just how much time Jesus spent eating. Most of Jesus' meals were shared with his inner circle, closest friends, and disciples, a couple of them even with the least popular characters in the New Testament. In these times, we see Jesus sharing his teachings and passing on his mission for the church on earth. After his resurrection, Jesus ate at least three meals with his disciples

---

1. University of Minnesota study, cited in August 2004 issue of *The Archives of Pediatrics & Adolescent Medicine*.

as a sign that he was truly risen from the dead and that his covenant with them remained (Jn 21:13-15).[2]

The early church also developed a powerful bond by eating together. "Every day they continued to meet together in the temple courts. They broke bread in their homes and ate together with glad and sincere hearts" (Acts 2:46).

Notice that there is no emphasis placed on what kind of food we should eat together, only that eating together has a way of bringing us "glad and sincere hearts." (Apart from bread and wine, there is no lasting record of the menu served at the Last Supper.) So it should come as no surprise that we've had some of our best conversations as a couple over pizza and beer. As a family, we have found that a big pot of pasta with a savory red sauce is the best way to get the kids to talk about their day at school and what happens to be especially important to them at the moment.

More delicious reasons to share a meal with your spouse:

Instant Check-in

Take the opportunity of a shared meal to learn something new about the other or just catch up on the news of the day. Talk about parenting styles, the news, what you're reading. Talk about your faith. We've found the following to be great dinner conversation starters:

---

2. *Everyday Life in Bible Times* by Arthur Klinck and Erich Kiehl. Concordia Publishing, 1995.

- Where would you like to retire someday?
- If you could visit anywhere in the world, where would you go?
- What is your least favorite kind of food?
- What do you imagine God is like?
- When you were growing up, who taught you most about God/your faith?

Improve Your Well-being

Meals together foster warmth, security, and love, as well as feelings of belonging. Planning meals, cooking, and eating together can be a unifying experience. Turn weeknight dinners into a shared activity. Take turns cleaning up; as our mothers used to say, "Many hands make light work."

Rekindle Romance

Since ancient times, some foods have been thought to have an aphrodisiac quality — spicy food, chocolate, red wine, fish, even snails. Today, it would seem that the kind of food you eat matters just as much as the quality time couples share when dining together. But intimacy is created through the shared laughter and conversation part of the meal, not so much the straw-berries dipped in chocolate. (On the other hand, if you've found a food that heats things up in your house, send it our way!)

Worries go down better with soup.
— JEWISH PROVERB

Save Money

While dining out can be a fun way to spend time together, it can also get expensive. Meals purchased away from home cost two to four times more than meals prepared at home. You'll be amazed at how much you save by limiting restaurant meals.

In times of stress, eating together can have a healing effect. (They don't call it "comfort food" for nothin'.) And while food is no substitute for love, it can be a great way to express empathy. Food is a way of caring for one another.

In times of great celebration or sadness, we eat. As Catholics, these meals often surround the sacraments. At weddings and funerals, baptisms and first Holy Communions, we eat. We eat together every Sunday at Mass when we share in the sacrificial meal of Christ. When someone dies, we bring food to the family as a symbol of our shared humanity and a sign of our mutual grieving.

This Wild Rice Soup recipe is our family's go-to meal in good times and bad. It's easy to make and serves a crowd. It tastes especially good when made with love.

Beth's Wild Rice Soup

1 can Canoe™ wild rice (usually found in the
   rice aisle)
2 cans cream of potato soup (can use low fat)
1 cup Velveeta™ cheese
1 small onion, chopped
1 ½ cups diced ham
4 cups half and half (can use light version)

Mix all of the ingredients together and let simmer in a crock pot or stock pot for several hours until it thickens. Flavor with pepper. Makes about 8 to 12 servings.

Take Away

Sharing meals together can be a unifying experience.

CHAPTER 8

Play

Come and Play...

> *Our wedding was many years ago. The celebration continues to this day.*
>
> — GENE PERRET

Successful marriages take work. (For the record, unsuccessful marriages take even more.) Kids, jobs, pets, families, money, sex, obligations — you name it — these things bring equal parts stress and joy to marriages. It's easy to lose sight of the joy in the day-to-day and focus only on the work.

Our culture places a lot of value on work. (Think about it: who's ever heard of a "playaholic"?) If the travel industry's research is to be believed, 47 percent of Americans give back vacation time every year, ostensibly so we can work more.

We're led to believe that play is childish. It's frivolous. Even when play is "tolerated," it's with the sneakers-and-sports-drinks mandate that we "Work hard, play hard."

Let's think hard before letting corporate America dictate how (and how intensely) we spend our free time. The truth is that recreation is just as critical for adults as it is for children. Don't apologize for it.

Stress-proof marriages know when to take a break and just have some *fun*. Marriages that have "lost their spark" often suffer just as much from a lack of play as from a lack of work.

> *The cure for boredom is curiosity. There is no cure for curiosity.*
>
> — DOROTHY PARKER

Here's a quick exercise:

Grab a pen and paper and sit down with your spouse. Without discussing it first, write down the date and time of the most recent thing you did together that you think both of you would qualify as "play." When you're finished, tell the other **just the date and time** you've written down. See if your spouse can guess the event you're recalling.

The objective is not to keep score about who can remember specific events, but rather, how close together are you in matching up activities you *both* would define as "play"?

If the dates you wrote down were more than a couple of weeks ago, it's probably time for the two of you to carve out more play time together soon.

Your Definition, Not Webster's

How we play in our marriages is really up to us. We will offer some ideas for activities you can try to infuse your marriage with a little fun, but it's just a laundry list of ideas. The prescription is to have some fun in your marriage, whatever that means to you.

The challenge in putting fun into a marriage may be finding those things that you both enjoy. Generally, the more things you can do that you both enjoy, the better. But don't rule out meeting in the middle. If one of you loves dancing or golfing, but the other is ambivalent, it might be worth the compromise. In those situations, though, remember the goal is to have fun. Activities that elicit sighing, eye rolling, or resentment probably fall into the category of "things we should do on our own."

It's a Date, Not a Grudge Match

It's probably a good idea to play for "fun" and not for "keeps." Maybe tennis is your thing as a couple. Or karaoke. And maybe healthy competition — even a little good-natured trash talk — gives your marriage a little zing. That's cool. Just remember: the goal is to have fun. Good sportsmanship is never more important than when we're competing for fun with our spouse. It's not about who wins or loses... but it just might end up being about who was a real jerk after totally dominating a round of mini golf.

> *It is for the purpose of flying that we rest.*
> — DOUGLAS JOHN HALL

Vacation

Whether you take off two weeks in the summertime and go someplace special or stitch together three- and four-day weekends, it's important to leave work behind and spend time as a couple (and as a family). Taking a vacation together, whatever that means for you, is good for your marriage. It decreases stress and allows for recreation and relaxation. Leave the laptop at home and explore a new city together. Or lie on the beach together and sip Daiquiris. (Deck chairs on your patio will do in a pinch.) It doesn't have to be fancy. Just remember to take a break from your normal routine and go on vacation. Together.

Home Games

Spending recreation time together doesn't have to be complicated or expensive. We know countless couples who stay in now and then on a Saturday night and play cards. Or Scrabble. Or Monopoly. Playing games together gives couples a chance to bring back some of the fun they enjoyed when first dating and serves as a reminder that there is more to life than reality television. Sure, playing together takes some effort, but you'll be amazed at what you can learn about your spouse in a good board game (like who insists on being the banker in Monopoly... you know who you are).

There Is No "I" in TEAM

Even if you're a nerdy couple like us, participating in a team activity is a great way to bond as a couple. From joining an intramural softball league to playing flag-football at your next family gathering, nothing reminds you that you're on the same team quite as much as actually *being on the same team*. Cheer for each other. Celebrate each other's strengths. Give high fives. It's fun to work together toward a shared goal. (Which is, of course, crushing the other team.)

Take Away

Healthy marriages build in time to play.

CHAPTER 9

Grow

Love Each Other for Who You Are . . . and for Who You Will Become

> *Don't smother each other. No one can grow in shade.*
> — LEO BUSCAGLIA

In a healthy marriage, it's important to leave room for both members to grow and change. As Barry and Emily McCarthy note in *Getting it Right the First Time*, "A vital marital task is to reach a balance between individuality and coupleness — between "me-ness" and "we-ness."[1]

Talk about how much time each of you is comfortable spending together, and how much time you need to spend alone. Spending time apart should not cause fear or anxiety in your marriage. If one partner is afraid of letting the other do things on his or her own, there may be some basic trust issues that need to be sorted out. Leaving spaces in your togetherness is a sign of solid and secure bond.

The strongest marriages are those in which both spouses are encouraged to pursue their own interests. One spouse may like to cook, while the other prefers to camp. One may be interested in a learning a foreign language, while the other has always wanted to learn to play

---

1. *Getting it Right the First Time* by Barry and Emily J. McCarthy. Taylor and Francis Group, 2004.

the guitar. While two become one in the spiritual sense, marriage does not mean that you are literally joined at the hip.

> *A good marriage is one which allows for change and growth in the individuals and in the way they express their love.*
>
> — PEARL S. BUCK

An elderly professor friend of ours used to tell us that he learned something new about his wife every day. In college we wondered how this could possibly be true. We've since learned that we can never completely know another human being. We change. Our life circumstances change. Human beings are always changing, always becoming something new.

Stuck in the Penalty Box

As time passes and a marriage matures, growth and change may be harder to achieve. It's easy to fall into the rut of work-home-dinner-sleep-work-home-dinner-sleep-work-home-dinner-sleep. And if you have little kids (like we do), it can be even more challenging to find the time for personal needs and interests. But it is important to do so. Mixing things up can be as simple as trying a new recipe or reading a good book before bed.

In our marriage, we have fallen prey to the dreaded pigeonhole. Our friends and families have pigeonholed us as the "academic couple." Our siblings have other roles. There is the "athletic couple" and the "party couple." We typecast couples and people, and then we find ourselves living up to that expectation. We recently mixed things up when we — the nerds — went to a pro hockey game and *loved it*. We proved that pigeon holes can get pretty cramped when occupied for too long.

One to Grow On

Over the years, we each have dabbled in new interests and activities. Some things have become woven into the very fabric of who we are as individuals, while others have gone by the wayside for lack of passion or practice. In any case, we have tried:

- Playing the guitar
- Studying a foreign language
- Earning a graduate degree in Theology
- Cooking
- Writing and producing plays
- Boxing
- Skating
- Writing a graphic novel
- Learning Pilates

That's just *our* list. Now it's your turn. Sit down with your spouse over dinner and talk about ways you've each grown and changed through the years. What new activities have you each tried? What stuck? What didn't? Did either of you find an unexpected passion or hidden talent? What are ways you can encourage each other's personal growth?

It's All about Me

The one caveat to leaving room for individual growth in your marriage is to be careful that you don't turn self possession into self-absorption. American society has always rewarded "rugged individualism" more than community — my own needs over the needs of the greater good — but a good marriage requires just the opposite. Whatever we do on our own should build up our marital bond, not tear it down.

Sometimes, individual activities and interests can be used as an escape from your marriage (not always a bad thing) or an excuse not to connect with your spouse (um, probably always a bad thing). You've got to honest about motivations and intentions for time apart. If one spouse's activity begins to cut into couple or family time and put strain on the relationship, it's worth exploring how things might be put into better balance.

Technology "Time Suck"

One final note about where time goes in a marriage. Many couples face the dilemma where one (or both) of you is spending an inordinate amount of time on the computer, whether that means spreadsheets, social networking sites, or chat rooms. It's essential to talk about what emotions are being fulfilled in the chat rooms that may be lacking in the relationship. While modern technology is amazing, it is no match for real, honest intimacy. It is too easy to keep secrets and lose time on the Web. This is just a passing glance at a subject that may bring up real issues in your marriage. Handle it with great care.

Take Away

Strong marriages strike a balance between "me time" and "we time."

CHAPTER 10

Laugh

So, a Husband and a Wife Walk into a Bar . . .

Laughter is the shortest distance between two people.
— VICTOR BORGE

It's become cliché to insist that laughter be a part of life. But there are few things more healing to a marriage than the ability to laugh.

While no definitive research exists on the health benefits of laughter, some scientists have taken a stab at identifying what it is about laughing that makes us feel so darned good.

In their hilariously titled paper "Psychophysiological Approaches to the Study of Laughter," published in the *Oxford Handbook of Methods in Positive Psychology*, authors Paul G. Devereaux and Kathi L. Heffner write that laughter has "specific and potentially health-relevant physiological effects on the central nervous, muscular, respiratory, endocrine, immune, and cardiovascular systems."

So, laughter is good for you. And like eating right and exercising, doing things that are good for your health is tantamount to doing things that are good for your marriage.

Holy Hilarity

As Catholics, we believe that Jesus was fully human as well as fully divine, and laughter is one of those delightful activities that is common to all humanity. And while there's no recorded evidence in the Gospels that Jesus actually laughed, he does stress the importance of joy. Surely Christ, more than any of us, understood that while life on earth can be filled with pain, grief, and sorrow, this life is also an occasion for great joy.

> *Jesus says, "I have told you this so that my joy may be in you and your joy may be complete."*
>
> — JN 15:11

Develop a Sense of Humor

Funny things happen in life and in marriage. If there's any doubt, just search "Wedding Bloopers" on YouTube, and try not to laugh. Cakes crash. Things start on fire. Point is, things are going to happen that are outside your control. In cases where there's nothing to be done for it, and no real tragedy has occurred, try to find the humor in the situation. Yes, it's cheap "T-shirt" psychology, but it has its place.

Most everyone has a sense of humor; we just find different things funny for different reasons. When life gets tense or things don't go our way, it's easy to get sullen and sulk and reject any attempt on the part of our spouse to lighten the situation with a little levity. What do we do when this happens in our house?

We moo at each other.

We really don't remember how it started, but we call it "The Humorless Cow." When one of us is refusing to have a sense of humor, the other will begin a quiet low that escalates into a full-throated moo. When done correctly, it is nearly impossible not to laugh at.

Find a signal in your marriage. (Yours doesn't have to be mooing.) Find a gentle way to remind each other that life is unpredictable, and its best moments include laughter. Laugh and help each other put things in perspective.

There's No Accounting for Taste

Having a sense of humor sometimes means swallowing pride. Sometimes it means being a good sport. Sometimes it means "taking a joke." What it means in all cases, though, is that you're willing to find something funny.

However, as mentioned previously, this is where the real trouble can start. Demanding that you each have a sense of humor is a far cry from insisting that you find funny everything I find funny. There are a handful of unbreakable laws of comedy, and the most important of them is this: Know Your Audience. One spouse's *New Yorker* cartoon is another spouse's knock-knock joke. Be attentive to what your spouse finds funny. If flushing the toilet while he's in the shower and making the water run cold is likely to get a laugh, go for it. If it's going to cause the fourth fight of the day and you're not even to breakfast yet, you might want to wait until he towels off.

But I Was Just Kidding!

Beyond simple taste is a larger issue of consideration. The goal is to make your spouse laugh. Better yet, to make the two of you laugh together. The point is laugh *with*, never laugh *at*. One-sided laughter is seldom good for a marriage.

In the spirit of keeping your marriage laughing, let's look at a couple surefire marital comedy killers:

Teasing

Teasing walks a very fine and dangerous line. Poking fun at one another's foibles can be charming. It can also easily tip over into passive-aggression. And if the person on the receiving end gets hurt, the teaser can always claim that the "teasee" needs to develop a sense of humor. Before you tease, check the intent and the content of what you're about to say.

Timing

There are times when you and your spouse will be around other people, and it will be tempting to make a joke or tell a story at your spouse's expense. It might even get a laugh — a huge laugh — and few things feel better than making a group burst out laughing. But this is another moment to check the content and intent of that killer anecdote you want to trot out at the company Christmas party. If your spouse is playing along, then all is well. But if you're getting signals that he or she is uncomfortable, it's better to abandon the story than to embarrass your better half.

Take Away

Laughing can help ease tension, put things in perspective, and bring you closer together.

Couples' Prayer

God of everlasting love,
help us to find new joy
in the face of routine,
to share our needs
with an open heart,
to acknowledge when
we have been wrong,
to forgive
as we have been forgiven,
to love as your Son, Jesus,
taught us to love.
Amen.